BRINGING OUT
ROLAND BARTHES

BRINGING OUT
ROLAND BARTHES

D. A. MILLER

UNIVERSITY OF CALIFORNIA PRESS

BERKELEY   LOS ANGELES   OXFORD

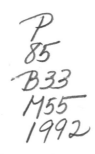

University of California Press
Berkeley and Los Angeles, California
University of California Press, Ltd.
Oxford, England
© 1992 by
The Regents of the University of California
Printed in the United States of America
9 8 7 6 5 4 3 2 1

*The author gratefully acknowledges the support of the Hyder E. Rollins
Publication Fund of Harvard University in the publication of this book.*

Library of Congress Cataloging-in-Publication Data

Miller, D. A., 1948–
    Bringing out Roland Barthes / D. A. Miller.
        p.   cm.
    ISBN 0-520-07948-5 (paper : alk. paper)
    1. Barthes, Roland.   2. Linguists—France—Biography.
3. Critics—France—Biography.   I. Title.
P85.B33M55   1992
410'.92—dc20
[B]   91-46420

BRINGING OUT
ROLAND BARTHES

To work out;—The sexual bias in
literary criticism. What sort of person
would the critic prefer to sleep with, in fact.

E. M. FORSTER, *Diary,*
25 October 1910

)

TWENTY YEARS AGO in Paris, long before I, how you say,
knew myself, a fellow student told me he had seen Roland Barthes late one evening at the Saint Germain Drugstore. Not the Americanized mini-mall where I would now
and then swallow much disgust to go satisfy my palate (also
Americanized, unfortunately for my ego syntony) with a
hamburger or an ice cream? But on reflection: what better
scene for Barthes to make than this curved, staggered dream
space, where the density of merchandise, marketing, and
anonymous masses of middle-class people must have pre-
sented so sharp a goad to his thinking about the status of
the sign in a consumer society? Although in frequenting the
Drugstore by night (as soon after this intelligence I began
to do), I may initially have hoped to see Barthes, I eventually
contented myself with *doing* Barthes, experiencing this pro-
miscuous emporium as I imagined he might. Now the various displays of luxury would provoke my hot imitation an-
ger with their repulsive evidence of bourgeois *myth* in the
process of naturalizing an oppressive class bias; now they
would lend themselves to my cool imitation appreciation as

3

so many relaxed *signifiers* stiffening in no hierarchy but the continually flexible one instituted by desire, whose only trajectory in any case conformed to the defiles of a labyrinth. I'm not sure when, how, or even whether I understood that others liked to loiter here of an evening quite as regularly as myself, but I gave up the habit—to do justice to the emphasis of my renunciation, one could say I kicked it— shortly after the moment when one such flâneur, who could hardly have been in a hurry, considering how many times I had already passed him, whose determination to be friendly on the contrary seemed to suppose all the leisure in the world, stopped me—*Monsieur!*—and said, almost as though it weren't a question at all, *avez-vous l'heure?*

IN BERKELEY, during the spring of 1988, when I now knew what time it was, or at any rate had become familiar with the *leurre* in such questions, I was preparing my first trip to Japan. Yet if I couldn't help taking Barthes's *Empire of Signs* as a point of departure (by no means the only one, or nearly so important as, for instance, my relation with Ben or Robert), this was mainly in the precise sense of *wanting to depart* from this text, from its armchair intellectual itinerary. My aggressive intention looked less to its proof in the course of beginning Japanese I had just completed, successfully enough to guarantee that unlike Barthes I wouldn't visit Japan altogether *sans paroles*, than in the Spartacus guide I had procured to help me explore the full extent of "gay Tokyo" permitted to fall under Western eyes. And since my knowledge of *kanji* was limited and Tokyo sidestreets tended in any case to go unmarked, I gave as high priority in my travel preparations to memorizing the landmarks of Shinjuku Ni-chome featured on the Spartacus map as to deciding which colors ("forbidden," as I liked to think of them, after Mishima), in which combinations, I might bring to wear on my sallies there, or to the hopeful acquisition of what Barthes had recognized for travelers as "the only lexicon that matters." Putting the edge on the sexual competence that I would feel as in Japanese however dubious I pronounced to myself the words for *type* (*taipu*), *cock* (*o-chinpo*), and *rubber* (*kondomu*), with some of the same exhilaration perhaps that Emma Bovary found in murmuring, "J'ai un amant, un amant," was my recollection of how impoverished Barthes's own practice of this lexicon appeared to be: *maybe, impossible, tired, I want to sleep* were the main possibilities he registered—only *headache* was lacking, I felt, to complete the pathetic picture of "the homosexual" (for once the sterilized, sterilizing term was apt) who in fact had no sexuality, in any sense that counted had no sex. So I was startled into fury when, rereading the *Empire* just before my departure, the better to gauge the distance I had already traveled from its jurisdiction, I saw that Barthes, in writing of those impromptu drawings by means of which the inhabitants of Tokyo give directions to strangers, illustrated the phenomenon with a sketch map of the same area of Shinjuku Ni-chome I had just committed to memory. *Siete voi qui?* I could have said with all the astonished rage of Dante Alighieri when he found his mentor Brunetto in that West Village bar.

OF THE MANY THINGS these two anecdotes may be made to mean, let me isolate the uncanniness with which I experienced the link between Barthes's writing and the practice, whether his or mine, of gay sexuality: as though of all things nothing could be odder in the course of shadowing this particular writer (of whose being *comme ça* I had nonetheless so old a knowledge that it preceded and doubtless even prepared the consciousness of my being "that way" too) than to be drawn into a company of hustlers—the same company to which I would later be shocked again on learning (in "Soirées de Paris") that Barthes himself used to resort; unless odder still was the utterly predictable operation of those laws of French farce decreeing that even in Tokyo's efficient love hotels I should glimpse through an open door across the corridor the very person I least expected to see, lounging, maybe even fiercely at it, with his partner on the futon. However intimately Barthes's writing proved its connection with gay sexuality, the link was so discreet that it seemed to emerge only in the coy or hapless intermittences of what under the circumstances I could hardly pretend to reduce to just his repression. What might it mean for me, lifting the repression, to notice and articulate this link for him? I plainly lacked the epistemo-erotic advantage enjoyed either by the nongay theorist of the closet (Sedgwick) or by the gay practitioner of outing (Signorile). Any knowledge I was able to produce of a "gay" Roland Barthes couldn't help being a knowledge *between us* and *of us both*, fashioned within the practices and relations, real and phantasmatic, of gay community, and across the various inflections given to such community by, for example, nation and generation. And so much the better: why, after all, had it come to interest me to know that Barthes—or any man for that matter—was gay, except for the reason that such information broached to fantasy the possibility of alleviating *an erotic pessimism* by producing with him, against him, a sexuality that had become "ours"? What I most sought, or what I most seek now, in the evidence of Roland Barthes's gayness is the opportunity it affords for staging this imaginary relation between us, between those lines on which we each in writing them may be thought to have put our bodies—for fashioning thus an intimacy with the writer whom (above all when it comes to writing) I otherwise can't touch. Barthes, of course, is some ten years dead, but who could ever think—in particular, at this date, what gay man—that someone's death ever stopped the elaboration of someone else's fantasy about him? (At Joe's house, after his burial, I looked for the copy of *A Lover's Discourse* that I had given him; it wasn't on its shelf. Had Joe, of all things always most unlikely, of all things once most desired, started to read it? Had he loaned, or outright given it to someone? to whom?) This essay proposes an album of moments—perhaps hardly even so complete as to be representative—in what journalism might call my "homosexual encounter" with Roland Barthes: responses to a handful of names, phrases, images, themes (whether or not strictly written by Barthes, all inscribed in his *text*) that happened to provide me occasions for assessing "between us" particular problems that must, as well as particular projects that might, inform a gay writing position. And though I mean to speak this encounter mostly in the form and idiom of *literary criticism*, there is no reason to suppose that so long and largely fantasized a relation, however chastened, will be at any moment exempt from the usual vicissitudes of adulation, aggression, ambivalence. Yet unless to bore or terrorize with a "positive image," neither perhaps can there be any reason to desire that exemption.

La Zambinella

Near the beginning of Balzac's "Sarrasine," at a party given by the Lanty family and amid speculation about the origin of their fortune, a philosopher goes so far as to say: "Even if the Count de Lanty had robbed a bank, I'd marry his daughter any time." To which the narrator of the story assents thus: "Who wouldn't have married Marianina, a girl of sixteen whose beauty embodied the fabled imaginings of the Eastern poets!" His punctuation, in abolishing the question that his grammar had begun to raise, alleges this certainty: *anyone* would have married so irresistible a girl. But supposing the passage were restored to the interrogative mode, two answers would surely impose themselves: for one thing, no woman *could* marry Marianina, nor is it at all sure, for another, that any man *would* whose sexual orientation failed to make him what is called the marrying kind. As it happens, the two figures the narrator overlooks in his exclamation of universal desire, the woman and the gay man, are also destined—more tellingly, if hardly more forcibly— to be elided in his narrative. Having revealed the object of Sarrasine's desire (La Zambinella) as a man in drag, and reduced the object of the narrator's (the Marquise de Roche- fide) to an auditor finally unwilling to hear another word, this ostensible story of grand heterosexual passion proves strangely short on women. Furthermore, with La Zambinella's transvestism tending (via the symbolism of his castration) to abolish itself in transsexuality, and Sarrasine bent only on being straight, a lack of gay men impedes it from becoming the homosexual love story that might have developed instead. A double paradox? Yet a single means in the story serves to repress both the woman and the gay man: the "femininity" that in their different ways (neither way having much to do with "masculine protest") both the Marquise and La Zambinella make the target of dissent. Having heard the story in which women never figure—are only figures—and that is supposed to seduce her into bed with the narrator, where she can play the only game in town with the only toy, the Marquise dismisses him by saying: "No one will have known me." Her claim reaches beyond the disingenuous psychology of her character (where it boasts the virtue supposedly never rewarded in Paris, a place that *quand même* hasn't exactly neglected her) to pass truer comment on the social structuration of her gender. Modern patriarchy is only capable of knowing her *either* through the various forms of femininity whose adroit manipulation by La Zambinella to such convincing effect on Sarrasine betrays their status as accessories in a drag show put on by men for themselves, *or*, in other words, as a castrato, a "woman" whose definitively "missing" or "diminished" penis presents *a contrario* proof of the intact grandeur of her self-deceived lover's. Yet because the femininity from which the Marquise knows she is alienated nonetheless remains the only theater "the world" concedes to her endeavors, her account of her situation ("You don't want me for myself") must oscillate between a radical feminist critique of the gender system and a conventional feminine gambit to get herself desired within it. Hence, too, her resentment (in this respect, quite unlike Sarrasine's) makes so little difference between the heterosexual and the gay man—both of whom after all reveal to her the male determinations of what, except as a masquerade, can hardly therefore be called "her" femininity—that at the same time as she shows the narrator the door, she echoes Sarrasine's own disgust for what she condemns as La Zambinella's "crime and infamy." By these terms, however, she can only mean such guilty acts as *his* wearing a dress, *his* getting fucked, *his* prostitution, and other like transgressions of what cultural codes have gendered as feminine. Accordingly, her repulsion commits her to reauthenticating—as a realization of her gender essence, not his—the femininity that, as soon as she reappears in the *Comédie humaine*, will have her back on the oppressive circuit she here fails to break.

The same femininity, though differently experienced, is no less crushing a burden for La Zambinella himself, who tremulously advances a proposition whose banality in no degree reduces its shock value: "And if I were not a woman?" His query is one that even today can hardly get a hearing—without at any rate resting on that devaluation of women from which, if it is ever to be properly understood, it needs most to keep its distance. The Zambinellian wish is not to detach male homosexuality from effeminacy (no suggestion here of a longing to be butch) but to disengage it from the double bind of that femininity to which our culture on the one hand obsessively remands it (for definition, understanding, representation) but on the other ruthlessly prevents it from laying the slightest legitimate claim, even in the concessive form of a "woman's prerogative." In New

York City once, at a certain Mexican restaurant, a man who seemed to be making himself amends for the mediocrity of its cooking with the excellence of its margaritas at last happened to spill one of them on my trousers, which occupied a seat at the table adjacent. When I failed to show adequate gratitude for his apology, he said to his dinner companion, another man: "She'll get over it." My "gay rage": not that I had been feminized, but that, *even so*, I was not entitled to a woman's concern for her clothes. The double bind presiding over the social construction of the gay man, in other words, is itself double: he must be, can't be, a man; he must be, can't be, a woman. That, in Balzac's story, is the all but unviable condition on which a man's gayness is allowed to become lived experience: and women like the Marquise who persuade themselves to resent a so-called appropriation of their feminine masquerade are as necessary to maintaining the suffering of this sufferance as men like Sarrasine who take their still more oppressive masculine masquerade for naturalist theatre. For the same reason, however, that the Marquise's defiant declaration ("No one will have known me") simultaneously implicates her in feminism and in the femininity that feminism would surpass, so La Zambinella's diffident query ("And if I were not a woman?"), uttered in "a soft silvery voice" that plays up to Sarrasine's eager will to misunderstand ("What a joke!"), gets retracted in the very course of being made into another performance, direct from La Cage aux Folles, of the homosexual as the false, failed, or defective woman. To the extent his performance may be taken to underwrite that patriarchal construction of the Woman as herself false, failed, or defective, as no better in short than her impersonator, then the female-inflected homophobia that will restore the Marquise to an oppressively "authentic" relation to her femininity chimes perfectly, if not harmoniously, with the gay-inflected misogyny that will keep La Zambinella in an oppressively "duplicitous" one to his own. The bouquet? That the evidence of hedging and infighting in the resistance to the modern gender system (evidence necessarily surfacing under a regime whose reach over the totality of social representation is equal to its grasp on subjects bound to imagine that any permanent desertion of their assigned places, however uncomfortable the latter, will leave them no other) affords to whoever wants to dismiss even the possibility of this resistance another occasion for general exclamation: No one will have known her all right! I'll bet he's no woman! "Who wouldn't have married Marianina!"

NEUTER

Despite the melodramatic explicitness with which "Sarrasine" situates the modern gay man in that double double bind which daily proves its utility to gender cops of both sexes, Barthes's analysis of the story in *S/Z* seems not even to recognize the pertinence of what in any case the spirit of his analysis would tend to dismiss as a mere homosexual thematics. It is worth recalling two complementary maneuvers through which our culture's general discourse promotes the negation of what, to respect its specific texture, one might call *gay material* when the latter threatens to migrate from the marginality where it normally makes its home: a *faux-naif* literalism to whose satisfaction gay material can never be conclusively "proven" to exist; and a prematurely sophisticated allegorization that absorbs this material under so-called larger concerns. Let these maneuvers be respectively exemplified, on the one hand, by the advice columnist for *Seventeen* magazine who reassures a young female correspondent that "the fact that [her friend] David is having fantasies about other men . . . does not necessarily mean that he is gay" without ever finding it desirable to inform her, however, that the fact might mean *precisely* that; and on the other by Susan Sontag claiming in *AIDS and Its Metaphors* that what inspires the neoconservatives' demagogic use of AIDS "is not just, or even principally, homophobia," the better to justify her total omission of any discussion of the homophobia that has nonetheless decisively structured AIDS-as-metaphor. In *S/Z*, the first maneuver reduces the gay material in "Sarrasine" to comparatively technical questions of narrative management. What Barthes's jargon dubs a *hermeneutic code* confines the question "And if I were not a woman?" (among whose reverberations we might otherwise have heard: can a man be homosexual? can a homosexual be a man?) to an entirely resolvable enigma centered on La Zambinella's biological gender. At the same time, a *proairetic code* makes La Zambinella's proposition disappear beneath its cover, so that far from issuing a discreet invitation to Sarrasine, he is simply declining the latter's love— and quite properly, since in this analysis (which uses its state-of-the-art technology here to rehearse an old naïveté) the fact that La Zambinella may not be a woman is tantamount to something as absolute as a physical limit or im-

13

pediment to his having sexual intercourse with another man. In the operation of the second maneuver, Barthes's general problematic of the *text* construes La Zambinella as nothing more or less than an instance of a classificatory disturbance, the local habitation and name of that hemorrhaging of meaning which tends to occur—to the great scandal of the bien-pensant guardians of the readerly, to the overwhelming delight of the avant-garde prolocutors of the writerly— when a binary opposition breaks down.

Though always the effect of homophobia, however, such disappearing acts are not always performed homophobically; inevitably, they have also been the recourse of gay people seeking to forestall homophobic attack. At Gold's, as soon as my set is over, I pass on the dumbbells (with great solicitousness—"Sure you got 'em, now?") to my boyfriend, who will in a moment return the favor; the acceptability, even the necessity, of the gesture to good gym form camouflages the most precious reason for performing it: that our fingers might briefly touch. Likewise, the gay male gender bind gets repressed by what Barthes would later call his "pseudo-linguistics," but only to get returned within their terminology as the neuter, a term whose emergence in *S/Z* as a major theme of Barthes's work owes at least as much to that gender bind as to any linguistic notion of neutralization. Its Zambinellian descent means that the Barthesian neuter can never exactly be ungendered or unsexed. It does not register a *general* deprivation of gender but the specifically *male* experience of such deprivation; still more important, neither does it restrict this deprivation to a loss of "masculinity," that is, to the dread castration by which the general imagination of the neuter is usually monopolized,* but makes no less definitive of itself a man's barred access to "femininity." If, however, grasped through its prehistory in "Sarrasine," the Barthesian neuter accurately transcribes the symbolic situation specific to gay men, it makes two important differences in doing so. First, it reverses the value signs. Instead of lamenting the lack of the masculine and the feminine, it celebrates its relief from their double-binding exigency. Of hard Zambinellian necessity Barthes makes his virtue, much as Sartre-sainted Genet wrested his identity from the curse the Others had laid on him. Second, conjoined with the pseudolinguistics that motivate its appearance, the neuter becomes the fulcrum of a general problematic, most concisely laid out in this passage from *Roland Barthes*: "Once the alternative is rejected (once the paradigm is blurred) utopia begins; meaning and sex become the object of a free play, at the heart of which the (polysemant) forms and the (sensual) practices, liberated from the binary prison, will achieve a state of infinite expansion. Thus may be born a Gongorian text and a happy sexuality."

It follows from the first difference that the neuter surpasses mere "reflection" to become a tactical notion; it follows from the second that this tactic has entrusted its own advancement to a certain protective coloring (its classic name being *discretion*) that to some extent must despecify its

---

*Consider how the two semantically opposed, morphologically identical words, *effeminate* and *emasculate* (in French *efféminé* and *émasculé*), instead of together defining a state of genderlessness, synonymously converge in a single attribute that may be predicated only of men.

gay bearing. Reading the neuter in Barthes—at any of its manifold sites, from the alternation of masculine and feminine pronouns in *A Lover's Discourse* to the account of his so-called migraines in *Roland Barthes*—means recognizing both the tactic and the ambivalence of the discretion by which the tactic "passes." Even at its most euphoric, the Barthesian neuter retains from its Zambinellian heritage a pained memory of "the binary prison" and "the intolerable scar of the paraded meaning, the oppressive meaning" that is strong enough to implicate the notion in a defense of the author's own body. (Barthes's headaches, he says, become his way of rendering his body, against that oppressive meaning, "opaque, stubborn, thick, *fallen*, which is to say ultimately [back to the major theme] neuter.") And even the neuter's broadest formulations are consistently linked to a specifically gay project of reclaiming, and gaining leverage against, a social symbolic "fate." Barthes develops the above program for a "happy sexuality," for instance, only and just after he has considered the melancholy case of a homosexuality that, for lack of "a neuter or complex term," would compel its practitioners to take their places once and for all within such heterosexualizing paradigms as active/passive, possessor/possessed, fucker/fucked. So, while that happy sexuality may be a paradise of indeterminacy, it can hardly be thought of as an indeterminate paradise.

Precisely when the discreet but discernible gay specificity of Barthes's text is ignored does this text present the most propitious occasion for rehearsing an antigay doxology. For in the guarding of that Open Secret which is still the mode of producing, transmitting, and receiving most discourse around homosexuality, the knowledge that plays dumb is exactly what permits the abuses of an ignorance that in fact knows full well what it is doing. Recognizing this logic must greatly diminish the persuasiveness of recent accounts (embraced by critics of both sexes, though—predictably—under the rules of a single sexuality) that equate the Barthesian neuter with a ruse for submerging, under general sexual indeterminacy, the specificity of women. Although such critics are demonstrably aware both of Barthes's gayness and of gay readings of Barthes's work, they see no reason to mediate their critique through articulation or even acknowledgment of the gender aporia that makes the social symbolic space allotted to gay men as impossible, as impassable, as perspective in Escher. However much in evidence, no other sexual difference in Barthes receives notice but the "good" kind he is charged with eliding. At best, therefore, the charge remains to be proven. At worst it can't help drawing an ease of proof from tacit collusion with that stereotyping of "the homosexual" which reduces all subtlety of analysis to merely echoing the detective in Balzac who, anticipating the bounden duty of our own gender police to demoralize any relation between women and gay men, says of Vautrin: "Apprenez ce secret: il n'aime pas les femmes."

To refuse to bring Barthes out consents to a homophobic reception of his work. But to accept the task? to agree to evincing the traces of a gay genealogy in a text whose even partial success in the culture's terms would almost guarantee (as with the accent of an ambitious provincial) the faintness of those traces? If "everything one does has to be paid for," as Wilde (who would know) has said, then the price of any *one's* attempting to undo what is a mass denial is the risk of his seeming—indeed, the certainty of his becoming—no less *mad* to the general view than the paranoid who seizes on Satanic verses anamorphosed in rock'n'roll lyrics. And this touch of madness is not the worst eventuality. In a culture that without ever ceasing to proliferate homosexual meaning knows how to confine it to a kind of false unconscious, as well in collectivities as in individuals, there is hardly a procedure for bringing out this meaning that doesn't itself look or feel like just more police entrapment. (Unless such, perhaps, were a *folie à deux*—where "two" stands for the possibility of community—that would bring it out in as subtle and flattering a fashion as, say, the color of a garment is said to bring out a complexion.)

The Goddess H.

What opposition more basic in Barthes's imagination, or central to his ethics, than between the Name and the Letter? The intense suffering Barthes alleges feeling "when he is named" overflows into his numerous complaints against the adjective, the image, the third person, the whodunit, all of which, for attempting to immobilize the signifying subject, are assimilated to the Name as an instrument of domination and death. In contrast, the Letter is always a good object for Barthes, cherished by him as the purity of a signifier that is "not yet compromised in any association and thus untouched by any Fall." Yet here too the Barthesian utopia is complicated by what it lets show of its own genealogy. If the letter-signifier appears empty, this is because it has been the site and is the result of an *evacuation*; its innocent airs never quite do away with the evidence of the semantic impressments that will already have left the smudge, precisely identifiable or not, of their prints. (Which is why, in Barthes's many encomia to the signifier, what he praises often looks less like purity than promiscuity—a proven ability to "fall" into an infinity of not always untraceable contacts.) On the M in Erté's alphabet, for instance, Barthes writes: "This inhuman letter (since it is no longer anthropomorphic) consists of fierce flames; it is a burning door devoured by wicks: the letter of love and death (at least in our Latin languages), flames alone amid so many letter-women (as we say Flower-Maidens), like the mortal absence of that body that Erté has made into the loveliest object imaginable: a script." On the one hand, in a patent allegory of Barthesian Writing, the letter advenes in a glorious (if also martyred) state of burning its bridges to a thus absented body—of literally, as French allows us to say, *burning its vessels*. Yet on the other, the passage's own writerly flagrancy (from the Latin *flagro*, to flare) fairly glows with the history, with the imaginary, of that body which—alone amid so many letter-women as Marcel within a budding grove, unique among them as Mother—has by no means therefore disappeared altogether in the flames. Indeed, so much flamboyance can hardly help kindling a suspicion that, not unlike the murderer in Agatha Christie who kills A and B to camouflage with the arbitrariness of the signifier his motives for the by no means arbitrary act of killing C, this incendiary text may be blazing the Letter's release from all verbal alignments by way of raising a smoke screen against one such alignment in particular: a certain name, perhaps, that the imprudence of divulging it consigns, like many another love letter, to the fire. On which conjecture, the writer fond of

Erté, *M.* COURTESY OF SEVENARTS LIMITED.

Arimondi, *Macho Man.* © ARIMONDI 551. USED WITH PERMISSION.

eliding himself into R. B., and his friends into A. C., E. B., D. F., will have been secretly banding, say with Shakespeare, as he is repeatedly supposed to have needed to conceal the identity of W. H.; say with Wilde, a character in whose *Dorian Gray*, when he likes people immensely, never tells their names to anyone; say with the entire long line of sodomites, inverts, homosexuals, and gay men to whom "safer sex" has ever had to mean, for themselves or their partners in crime, securing an incognito.

On at least one occasion, the euphoria arising from the Letter expressly acknowledges the extent of its determination by such distinctively gay experience of anonymity. In a handwritten preparatory note for *Roland Barthes*, photographically reproduced in the published text, its author describes a goddess he calls "Homosexuality" or "Homo," who permits him to say, do, understand, know so much that she becomes a catalyst, a mediator, a figure of intercession. The note is apparently an earlier version of the following passage in the finished text, now entitled simply "The goddess H.": "The pleasure potential of a perversion (in this case, that of the two H's: homosexuality and hashish) is always underestimated. Law, Science, the Doxa refuse to understand that perversion, quite simply, *makes happy*; or to be more specific, it produces a *more*: I am more sensitive, more perceptive, more loquacious, more amused, etc.—and it is this *more* where we find the difference (and consequently, the Text of life, life-as-text). Henceforth, it is a goddess, a figure that can be invoked, a means of intercession." Observe how "the goddess Homosexuality" or "Homo" gets enfolded into "the goddess H.," where H, as a relatively emancipated signifier, can then unfold into a plurality of perversions, among which homosexuality, even "in this case," has lost its priority (lost too, perhaps, the pain of that priority, as when once, not long ago, by way of cutting a man down to size, a size at any rate smaller than the unwieldy one he had grown to in my heart, I took to referring to him by his first initial, which was also that of two close friends). In the movement from the Name (as meaning *that name*) to the Letter (as meaning, only possibly, that name *among others*)—more accurately, in the oblique but observable *proffering* of the movement—consists the whole figured relation of Barthes's writing to his homosexuality. Or nearly: for Barthes will later inform us that for reasons of health he has never been able to enjoy smoking hashish.

As this pattern would predict, Barthes's relation to the act of gay self-nomination proves nothing short of phobic. "To proclaim yourself something is always to speak at the behest of a vengeful Other, to enter into his discourse, to argue with him, to seek from him a scrap of identity. 'You are . . .' 'Yes, I am . . .' Ultimately, the attribute is of no importance; what society will not tolerate is that I should be . . . *nothing*, or that the something that I am should be openly expressed as provisional, revocable, insignificant, inessential, in a word, irrelevant. Just say, 'I am,' and you will be socially saved." The quasi-paranoid mistrust finds its warrant in the undeniable fact that, as a general social designation, the term *gay* serves a mainly administrative function, whether what is being administered is an insurance company, a marketing campaign, a love life, or a well-orchestrated liberal dinner party—as a result of which, even men on whom the overall effect of coming out has been empowering will sometimes also have to submit to being mortified by their membership in a denomination that general social usage treats, as though there were nothing else to say about them, or nothing else to hear them say, with all the finality of a verdict. (How well an arduously *sympathetic* investment in the category of gay men can facilitate a managerial anxiety to place them, or still less lovely, to show them their place, I eventually learned from Mona, whose last Christmas present to me was an organizer.) Yet gayness hardly operates in the manner of just any socially assigned attribute. What is still most familiarly solicited from the devotees of this proverbially innominate love, or solicited from others *for* them, is not a name, but the continual elision of one. (Consider: —Funny guy, that Al. He's fifty years old and never been married. —Maybe he's gay, Dad. —I didn't say *that*.) To the proclamation of gayness whose address, in any case, the Vengeful Other who sneers "You are" is obliged to share with the Kindly One who smiles "I am too," society continues to prefer the sotto voce stammering of a homosexuality from which nothing in fact is more tolerated, more desired, than that it be *provisional* ("it's just a stage"), *revocable* ("keep your options open"), *insignificant* ("it doesn't necessarily mean"), *inessential* ("are you sure?"), and, under the cumulative weight of all these attributes, expulsively *irrelevant*. Like the celebrity or politician whose refusal to discuss his sexuality (as being at once too marginal to bear on his business in the world and too central to forego full benefit of his right to privacy) declares that sexuality as legibly—I don't say with as much charm— as any sage nylon jacket ever did; or like those old-fashioned gay rendezvous, which are always more than sufficiently well identified by the mere emphatic vagueness of their

names (such as, in Paris: L'Insolite, Le Curieux, Le Camé-
léon, and so on); so Barthes never with greater docility takes
on a prescribed social identity than here in his ostensible
argument against doing so. Even supposing a single indi-
vidual refusal of a name could arrest the whole social process of nomination by which names are given out, it would
remain the case that when the name in question is *that name*,
whose most diffuse prejudicial effects depend on its *not*
being pronounced—on its being restricted, quasi-
catachrestically, to a system of connotation—then silence,
far from guarding a subject against these effects, would leave
him all the more destitute of resources for resisting them. If
Barthes's reticence has successfully shielded anyone, it is his
homophobic critics, who are spared having to show how
deeply their attacks are motivated by a name he never
claims.

Yet how would homophobia know enough to strike, except by relying on information from a more reliable and less
arid source in Barthes's writing than the proclamation that
the author has merely *decided* not to make? Even when not
spoken about in this writing, homosexuality does not fail to
be spoken any the less. On the contrary, though seldom a
topic, it comes to inflect every topic, no matter how remote,
through the operation of a means comparable, even contin-
uous, with that inexhaustible fountain of revelation popu-
larly known (in fear, scorn, or love) as *a gay voice*. (In a
former life, when I used to stand in dread of hearing myself
on a tape recorder, I could not have imagined how often now
I listen to messages on my answering machine solely in
hopes of hearing an instance of this voice, for the pleasure
of playing it back.) That such inflection only works by mo-

bilizing highly variable and in any case never quite provable connotations makes a difficult task of specifying how, or as what, it is perceptible, except, grosso modo, by reference to the state of general opinion that is always ready to suspect, and often actually able to detect, male homosexual behavior in even the minutest deviation, by dilation or intensification, from male homosocial norms. The glance becomes one of "the signs" as soon as it seems to linger; the handshake, when it isn't punctual enough in relinquishing its hold; and similarly with the *négligé* that betrays no neglect, or the voice that instead of expediting the pleasure it takes in your company tends to draw it out in a kind of otiose sigh. Barthes takes less and less care to keep the same principle from casting on his prose, almost simply by virtue of a thing known as *manner*, the shadow of being "too pretty for a man's" (in alternative codes: too light, coy, sentimental, precious) to the point where among these codes, Barthes's own name has come to be included—or so I caught the drift of the reviewer who complained that my mentors were "people like Barthes." Moreover, though Barthes is plainly more conscious and conducive of his manner than most people are of their voices, yet to the degree that it manifests that nonpersonal individuality he likes calling *grain*, he may not be much more in command of it. Under usual conditions of reception, at any rate, such incorrigibility can't help approximating that of a certain voice in putting the ins and outs of the closet beyond power of election.*

---

*Guy Scarpetta, having visited Barthes's seminar, recorded this impression: "I was at once struck by the marked contrast between his words and

With increasing visibility after *S/Z*, Barthes is engaged in the ambiguously twinned projects of at once sublimating gay content and undoing the sublimation in the practice of what he calls in the case of Proust "inversion—*as form*." In Barthes's characteristic argument, be it mandarin or merely panic-stricken, the force of *that name* (already somewhat despecified as Pleasure, Perversion, Fashion, the Body) tends to surrender to the generality of an all-absorbing paradigm (of Language, Writing, the Text); in his characteristic performance, this paradigm becomes itself an erotic, perverse, dandiacal embodiment, as though it liked nothing better than to relapse into the favorite themes whose particular bias is *persistent enough* not only to prevent the realization of a successful *Aufhebung* but even to make the whole wobbly dialectic apparatus start to look like a perverse erotic enhancer. If pleasure, for instance, is obliged for its expression to become—how unpromisingly!—a pleasure "of the text," the text is free to develop in the process a sexuality so accommodatingly perverse that only the boldest bad faith could think it had anything in common with the censorious notion of "the pleasure of reading." Similarly, an interest in fashion can only take the form of *The Fashion System*,

---

his voice. Albeit the content of his discourse was abstract, semiological, 'scientific,' the voice itself never ceased being eroticized: warm, deep, slow-paced, cajoling, velvety, modulated (Casals playing Bach on the cello): it was with his voice that he would cruise. I immediately sensed that most of his auditors, male and female, so intensely submitted to the charm (the 'obtuse meaning') of this voice that they ended by savoring it for itself, almost independently of what it said. A kind of 'extra,' this voice grazed them, disturbed them, enveloped them, seduced them—to the point of excitation pure and simple."

which, however, precisely in that it hasn't worn well, makes a good index of how thoroughly modish its structuralist systematicity once was. At least until "Soirées de Paris," what one might call the (poignant, exasperating) hysteria of Barthes's most invidiously written texts lies in the activity of this contradiction—that while they phobically sacrifice homosexuality-as-signified, leaving the appeased deity of *general theory* as fixed as ever in its white-male-heterosexual orientation, they happily cultivate homosexuality-as-signifier, wreaking havoc on the discursive sobriety that works better than anything to give such coordinates an ecumenical air. No wonder Barthes ceased to be taken seriously as a theorist during the very period when his work most fully emitted that resonance of the body which *Writing Degree Zero* had earlier called *style*: who could recognize theory once it enjoined the necessity of looking at its ass in the mirror?

Two Bodies

During my first year at Yale I discovered this truth, whose *longue durée* Richard would confirm there eighteen years later: namely, that the entitled man, or the boy aspirant to entitlement, is less inclined to contour his genitals in briefs than to make them invisible in boxer shorts. A twice obnoxious preference, it now seems to me: on the one hand, a presumptuous discourse of procreative sexuality, testicular "freedom" always being earnestly sanctioned by its beneficial effect on the production of fertile sperm; on the other, an immodest practice of hiding the penis, which disappears into a cool rectangularity that (already anticipating the *suit* that is such underwear's "logical" and ethical extension) only apotheosizes it as the phallus. In boxer shorts, a man no longer has a dick; he becomes one.

This truth will also be familiar to readers of the nineteenth-century novel, where a prerequisite for the success of the ambitious young man from the provinces is the course in body *Bildung* that instructs him on how to withdraw from the pleasures and dangers of visibility, from an *object* position where he might be desired, circulated, wounded. In the canonical story of making it, Balzac's *Père Goriot*, Rastignac requires a body whose power and prestige depends on its vanishing into a gaze that cannot effectively be returned. What Balzac calls Rastignac's "aplomb" (his perpendicularity, his straightness) comes from his submitting his body to correction, to its most profitable sociosexual appropriation and disposition. He needs, for example, to dress for the success that he seeks, as the text aptly notes, *à corps perdu*, for along with his illusions, it is precisely his body—as a host of pleasures—that he must sacrifice, whether that loss be connoted in the mutilating work of the tailor through whose help he cuts, in the end, only a figure; in the bondage of a tie that, even before anyone shows him the ropes, he knows to wear high on the throat; or in the imperforate ideal reflected in the highly polished surface of his boots. For what is eventually arrested along with Vautrin is not just the explicit homoeroticism that circulates in and as the narrative around Rastignac's body, but also, more important, the pleasurable visibility of the male body as such. That visibility spells capture as directly as Vautrin's arrest follows on the denuding of his muscular torso, on the revelation of those "fatal letters" of identification which—*Père Goriot* continues being written in our own American day— have been branded on his broad shoulders. In contrast, by the time of Rastignac's final appearance in the novel, he is visible only as vision itself: hidden in the failing light, he surveys from the heights of Père Lachaise the good things of a world that he is thus enabled to "pump" and "penetrate."

In a culture that since the eighteenth century has massively depreciated male embodiment—as Elaine Scarry reminds us via Marx, it is not the capitalist, but only the worker, who "suffers, desires, and risks in his body"—we must register the distinctiveness of those practices of post-Stonewall gay male culture whose explicit aim, uncompromised by vicissitudes of weather or fashion, is to make the male body visible to desire. The men of the Muscle System or the Chelsea Gym, who valuing tone and definition over mass give as much attention to abs and glutes as to pecs and lats; who array their bodies in tanks and polos, purchased when necessary in the boys' department, in Spandex and Speedos, in preshrunk, reshrunk, and, with artisanal care, perhaps even sandpapered 501s—let us hail these men (why not by the name given during the Directoire to the women who dampened their that much more dramatically clinging gowns: *les merveilleuses?*) for lending whatever inchoate social energies would resist the boxer shorts ethic the brave assistance of an advance guard that proceeds insensible to the pompous charges of exhibitionism, or hectoring accusations of body terrorism, thrown in the way. No doubt it would hardly be altogether possible to sever male embodiment from the obvious, obviously troublesome, ambiguities that attend macho fantasy about the male body (as *the body that can fuck you, fuck you over*). In some degree this fantasy determines for men and women alike the perception and experience (as attractive, repulsive, dangerous) of the male body in our culture. But it would be just as untenable to turn gay men's collective refusal, as it were, *to closet their bodies* into merely another manifestation of such fantasy, as though the latter's power were such as could even eventually make every sissy the "man" that his father—under the uneasy impression, however, that another choice was possible— may have exhorted him to *be*. Only those who can't tell elbow from ass will confuse the different priorities of the macho straight male body and the so-called gym-body of gay male culture. The first deploys its heft as a *tool* (for work, for its potential and actual intimidation of other, weaker men or of women)—as both an armored body and a body wholly given over to utility, it is ultimately aligned with the unseen body of its bossman, the dick in boxer shorts and business suit; whereas the second displays its muscle primarily in terms of an *image* openly appealing to, and deliberately courting the possibility of being shivered by, someone else's desire. Even the most macho gay image tends to modify cultural fantasy about the male body if only by suspending the main response that the armored body seems developed to induce: if this is still *the body that can fuck you, etc.*, it is no longer—quite the contrary—*the body you don't fuck with*.

Though Barthes's own emphasis on the body runs little risk of being confounded with an ideal of physical culture, it belongs to the same gay male cultural project of resurrecting the flesh, to which it adds (or in which it brings out)

certain valuable nuances. For the economic system that suits
an empowered subject to the logic of capital will also tend
to correlate an embodied subject with the status of a com-
modity. To the extent that gay male embodiment may be
seen to amount to the normativeness of a single body
type—a view perhaps only possible from the steamed up
windows of a tour bus doing Castro Street, or from similar,
if more influential, perspectives in advertising and the me-
dia—then it stands contradicted by an abstraction that continues to alienate everyone from their bodies, including
those who apparently come closest to embodying the types.
Against such an abstraction, Barthes's promotion of the
body, without at all failing to insist on the body's material
lovability, is moved to conceive this body in its most em-
barrassed state, devoid of anything that might be called "fin-
ish." "To write the body" means writing "neither the skin,
nor the muscles, nor the bones, nor the nerves, but the rest:
an awkward, fibrous, shaggy, ravelled thing, a clown's coat."

Consider, then, in *Roland Barthes*, the photograph of
Barthes as a child being held by his mother. The universalization attempted by his Lacanian caption—"The demand
for love"—hardly succeeds in pacifying the scandal of this
amazing image, in keeping it from being read (no less, or
less certainly, than anything in Mapplethorpe) as the image
of a certain gay male body. His ungainly lower limbs betray
the boy, and not just because, as Barthes says of studio por-
traiture, "every ideal image, every social promotion begins
by getting rid of the legs." They are too long for short pants,
and too long to justify what the boy nonetheless evidently
persists in wanting: to be carried by his mother. "But isn't
it time he stood on his own two feet?" etc. Worst of all, the

adult Barthes, far from having the sense to be ashamed of his prolonged dependency, matter-of-factly proffers and "assumes" this evidence of his body's id, just as, with great and deliberate simplicity, he will later mourn his mother's death in perfect indifference to all charges of "overattachment." In fact, every image of Barthes, whether fully grown or all alone, materially reinscribes his mother in the characteristically dejected posture of his body, always ducking and drooping, as though always wanting, but never any longer able, to drop into her arms. (The prospect of that languid *retombée* is what most whets Barthesian eros, whose utopia lies beyond the heroics of erection, beyond even the splurges of *jouissance*, in the recovery of "sexual quiescence." When he is alone in an elevator with a man, his first gesture after kissing him is to rest his head on his shoulder.) Openly displaying and freely discoursing of his mothered body, Barthes shares with, say, the clone whose much different body is devoted to signaling its various sexual availabilities this common refusal: of the desirability, even the possibility, of the male body's *autonomy*. (So it is that Barthes's grief over his mother's death can speak to the clone's comparably all-affecting depression by the devastation of his once flourishing culture.)

JAPANESE EYES

To the mystery of Eric's appeal with other gay men, whose source I had found as puzzling as its effects were beyond dispute, Robert confidently propounded this key: the size of his cock. Attempting to disqualify so coarse an explanation,

"The demand for love" *[Roland Barthes with his mother].*

Robert Mapplethorpe, *Brian Ridley and Lyle Heeter*. © ESTATE OF
ROBERT MAPPLETHORPE. USED WITH PERMISSION.

I had recourse to skepticism: and how could he, hardly more intimate with Eric than I, know *that?* In the course of enumerating inferences drawn variously from Eric's ethnicity, body type, and so forth, he interrupted himself, plainly exasperated with this mode of reasoning and with the interlocutor who seemed to require it—"David: *you have to look.*"

Barthes's writing practice is never more directly provocative of our thinking about the inscription of the body than when in *Empire of Signs* he dares to look the Japanese *in the eye*, the eye that has been the favored referent of racist insult to the bodies of Japanese and other Asian people. Now the white Western liberal characteristically refrains from taking any notice whatever of the racially other's body, under the assumption that no such notice *can* be taken without repeating or in some way reinforcing the abusive mythologization of this body. With this paradoxical result: the white Western liberal respect for the racially other takes the form of *denying* his body, whose specificities are surrendered without a struggle to the racism that is, for its part, more than willing to describe this body concretely, but only, in deriding it, to justify the often institutionalized cultural aggression against it. (As early as *Mythologies* Barthes noted the poverty of myth on the Left, which, as a result, he claimed, could never take hold of "the vast surface of 'insignificant' ideology" on which human relationships are inscribed in everyday life.) In its willingness to write on the very site of racist stereotype, then, Barthes's text on "the Japanese eye" also breaks with the liberal reticence whose embarrassment unwittingly assents to that stereotype. Any attempt to make the operation of Barthes's sexuality peripheral to this initiative would be simply to let another version of such reticence fall on the difference of the other. Entirely devoid of that liberal advocacy which in defending "them" is even more concerned to establish the advocate's own humanity, Barthes writes out of his patent pleasure in Japanese bodies, faces, eyes, on which he bestows his own look of love. This inevitably means that the Japanese eye gets configured in terms of *writing*—that is, as an instance of a cherished signifying process that no meaning can ever annul or arrest. "Calligraphed" into the anatomy like an ideographic character, according to a model that is "not sculptural but scriptural," this eye suspends "moral hierarchy" and embodies "the non-secret relation of a surface and its lines"; it holds out the possibility of a euphoria arising not only from "that gap, that difference, that syncope which are . . . the open form of pleasure," but also, following the drift of Barthesian eros already noted, from the promise of a certain detente (as it were *afterwards*) made in the ease of the eye's "descent into sleep."

Such "writing," in which Barthes's own writing practice coincidentally finds its ideal, does not exactly confer an interpretation on Japanese eyes, in the sense of fixing them in some decided and easily circulable meaning that could scarcely fail at being an instrument of domination. Nor does it quite precipitate a description of these eyes, by way of telling us what they look like. To an essentially *plastic* orientation from which the aesthetic act of composing the racially other's body merely provides consolation, not to say justification, for a less pretty cultural tendency to consider it disposable, Barthes's text prefers a continual modulation of the signifier, an ongoing displacement of terms, that *en passant* lightens all weight, reduces all viscosity, of attribution. (A certain humiliated sense of my own eyes was revoked the moment Anita produced for me *another word* than I habitually used to describe them: a word that, so to speak, only glanced at them.) One may of course wish to find in the refusal of interpretation a vestigially recycled myth of inscrutability, and in the refusal of description the characteristic denial of fetishism; but in doing so, one may also wish to reflect on the tendency of such discoveries to reaffirm the irresistible character of the racist imaginary, to which a certain zeal in recognizing its signs might be thought to submit as well.

Writing the Japanese eye that is itself writing, Barthes enunciates an ethic whose first address may be best thought of as those gay men, including himself, whose intimacies traverse, and are crossed by, the white Western construction of race. Their pleasure *and its condition*, far from being repressed or masked, become the visibly active motive of a discourse that seeks to do something more than just attest to the inevitability of "sex" between races. In the case at hand, the fundamental desire of this discourse might almost seem anticipated by the economic—hence already more than economic—power of Japan to get itself figured in Western discourse as that nonwhite, non-Western country on which it is possible to bestow *a lateral gaze*, as between equals. That gaze is what Barthes seeks, deploys in looking at the Japanese eye, which is painted like a "comma sideways"—or as his French has it, "couchée," reminding us how the possibility of this laterality *and of its implied reciprocation* is doubled in a homosexuality that by definition neutralizes the gender hierarchy, and so is well disposed to dreaming that it might suspend the operation of other hierarchies too. (John, taller than I, was never more charming than in reassuring me: "That's what beds are to adjust for.")

Yet however necessary dreaming laterality must be to realizing it, that very necessity must make it to some degree a utopian projection—a cease-fire declared in the midst of hostilities that do not thus simply cease. Every utopia secretes signs of the conflict that it fulfils the wish to abolish; these signs must be read so long as utopian vision animates, rather than replaces, a labor of bringing it to pass. Here, the problematic extent of utopian extrapolation may be measured by the distance between two images coinhabiting the same page of *Empire of Signs*. One is a photograph that appeared in a Japanese newspaper of Barthes himself, "eyes elongated, pupils blackened by Nipponese typography"; the other is a glossy studio portrait of the Japanese actor, Teturo Tanba, who "'citing' Anthony Perkins, has lost his Asiatic eyes." Barthes's Japanned eyes meet Tanba's Westernized ones in what seems given to us as a literally perfect, because perfectly literal, exchange of glances. Yet this pacifist phantasmagoria of "an eye for an eye" would fade considerably from any view that got close enough to see the *whites* of those eyes—see, that is, how the equal status of trading partners is belied by Tanba's blepharoplasty, a surgical operation on the actor's body to which merely doctoring Barthes's photograph is hardly the equivalent, except to the postmodern sensibility that never seems more imperially Western than when Barthes lightly appeals to it ("what then is our face if not a 'citation'?") to pass over the evident preponderance of Western body norms.

It is not then a matter of saving Barthes's text from its

This Western lecturer, as soon as he is "cited" by the *Kobe Shinbun*, finds himself "Japanned," eyes elongated, pupils blackened by Nipponese typography.

ロラン・バルト氏

遺文化使節として来日した。二十
日まで滞在し、その間東大、京
大など数カ所で講演を行なう予定
である。

人文科学を駆使

バルトの名前は日本ではほとん
ど知られていない。（処女作「文
体＝エクリチュール＝の原点」が
森本和夫氏によって「零度の文

しかし、い
ティックな管
トはフランス
「問題の」批
るだろう。前
シュレ論」「一
ー又論」「批
論」「批評と
これまでの著

Whereas the young actor Teturo Tanba, "citing" Anthony Perkins, has lost his Asiatic eyes. What then is our face, if not a "citation"?

inscription in power by means of its inscription in pleasure, or vice versa, but of securing for the discussion of his text a recognition of the extent to which pleasure and power invest *every* representational project and writing position. The numerous accounts produced for the American public over the past decade concerning "the challenge" of that offense-giving oxymoron, the "Japanese giant," are at least as abundant in fantasies about the Japanese body as *Empire of Signs*. But these fantasies, never willing or obliged to be recognized as such, are commensurately less available for being negotiated, even as they implicate both partners in a far more volatile erotics. Recall this aspect of Jesse Helms's disapprobation of certain famous Mapplethorpe photographs: they are *not racist enough*. "There's a big difference between *The Merchant of Venice* and a photograph of two men of different races . . . on a marble-top table." And he is right; an anti-Semitic representation, even unsigned by Shakespeare, *is* so much more at home in our culture than an image of black and white men together—whether or not in embracing they go so far as to desecrate the more acceptably mottled centerpiece of the middle-class living room—that it would be premature to reduce the force and value of such an image to whatever reservations are difficult not to have about Mapplethorpe's falsely serene classicism as it encounters black men's bodies. Furthermore, as Helms's heavy breathing would make clear even if the photograph in question actually existed (which it does not), the senator had already amply and intensively imagined the sexual possibilities between men "of different races" long before he ever heard the name of Mapplethorpe or metathesized that name into the fantasy—evidently too hot to handle by any but the most projective touch—of a hard-as-marble top. A would-be prudent silence about the other's body never means that differences between races (or classes, or genders, including the "neuter") cease at any moment being thought, fantasized, eroticized, *spoken*: it merely deprives such differences of any tradition of articulation but the most ponderous (immobilizing, intractable) one engrossed by bigotry. Between that loud-mouthed discourse and frigid liberal silence, gay men of course know a kind of third term—by which I refer to that fascinated discourse on the male body informally but incessantly spoken in bars and bedrooms, between lovers or about them between friends, a discourse that with its meticulous observation and multiple fetishizing articulates the most casual cruise. If by virtue of its exceptionally nuanced attention such *discours amoureux* can hardly fail to observe the features that are counted for race, neither can it help producing more and finer discriminations than that kind of discrimination—simplist, self-evident, final—ever knows what to do with. I owe to this generous (forebearing as well as abundant) discourse the fact that I was twice mistaken for Yoshi, once by Eddy at the gym, a second time much later by Yoshi himself, as we went over a photograph album together. The first occasion was spoiled for me by the ready-to-hand jocularity of those who heard Eddy make his mistake, or later recount it; under the rule that no more recognizes resemblance across race than difference within it, Eddy's famously sharp eyes could only be thought to have had a vision. With the second instance, partly because of the same blue-plate dispensation, I know even less than I did at the time how to give my gratification a decent countenance.

THE NOVELESQUE

An incident from Barthes's life, recounted by him as though it had befallen someone else, offers me a reason why I always cry at weddings: "Walking through the Church of Saint Sulpice and happening to witness the end of a wedding, he has a feeling of exclusion. Now why this faltering, produced under the effect of the silliest of spectacles: ceremonial, religious, conjugal, and petit bourgeois (it was not a large wedding)? Chance had produced that rare moment in which the whole Symbolic accumulates and forces the body to yield. He had received in a single gust all those divisions of which he is the object, as if suddenly, it was the very *being* of exclusion with which he had been bludgeoned, dense and hard." Of "all those divisions," the one between hetero- and homo- by so far best explicates the affect and figuration of the experience as once again to blow the cover of Barthes's ostensibly impartial plural. To that degree, no doubt, the passage will strike some as being conducted, for all the manifest sophistication of its prose, in the naïvely absurdist manner of the tabloid press: GAY MAN BATTERED IN CHURCH BY WEDDING CEREMONY. Yet Barthes will be judged to be overreacting only on the same principle that, in the eyes of the straight couples who get to wear their sexuality, as he elsewhere puts it, "like the Legion of Honor ribbon in a buttonhole," the gay couples giving the least sign of their own will appear to be inexcusably flaunting it. Unlike the current linguistic habit of inflating repeated criticism of anything or anybody into a "bashing" (of which the most cognizant example must be the charge of "Catholic-bashing" leveled at opponents to Church teaching on sexuality by so keen a propagandist for the homophobic cause as John Cardinal O'Connor), Barthes's metaphor of being bludgeoned does not despecify and trivialize the increasing literal violence against gay people. On the contrary, with a kind of unwitting militantism, it breaks with the usual habit of underestimating that violence, whose extent it refuses to restrict to the most openly brutal instances, or to the geography, class, and age group of those most likely to perpetrate them, recognizing instead how such instances are all but licensed in social structure and symbolic order to the point where every wedding, every public exhibition of heterosexual impulse (or compulsion) assents to an entitlement that is secured, and made to signify, precisely through and against its homophobic exclusions.

Furthermore, if Barthes falters, it is that the spectacle of this entitlement involves him in a "final alienation: that of his language: he could not assume his distress in the very code of distress, i.e., *express* it." Though he goes on to regret not having a *lyrical* language at his command, his dispossession—evoked lyrically enough, after all—has demonstrably more to do with restricted access to *narrative*. For while he is only permitted to lay claim to a slight, nearly ineffable incident, the couple is in full and open possession of a story, a story, moreover, that one hardly exaggerates in our culture to call *the* story. Outside the heterosexual themes of marriage and the oedipalized family (the former linked to the latter as its means of transmission), the plots of bourgeois life, and of the classic bourgeois fiction that, via Hollywood, continues to provide models for that life, would all be pretty much unthinkable; as Barthes himself observes later in the same text, "If we managed to suppress the Oedipus complex and marriage, what would be left for us to *tell?*" Hard and dense with its own eroticizable authority, the observation can't but be understood as redressing the abashed breakdown of utterance in Saint Sulpice—of which sufficient vestige remains, however, to shade the luminous assurance of a simple rhetorical question with the genuine puzzlement of a koan over which every gay subject is obliged to ponder: so long as narrative is wedded to marriage and kin to the family, what *is* left for us to tell? *David Copperfield* lets us take the classic dimensions of this predicament with David's inability—remarkable in someone supposedly adept at the usages of the Victorian novel—to confer a story line on the several homoerotic incidents of his adolescence; like Steerforth sleeping in the moonlight, or David awake watching him, these just lie there. Nor do the dismal more recent efforts to "homosexualize" our culture's omnipresent marriage plot with stories of boy meeting boy, or girl getting girl, suggest that its heterosexist bias is at all corrigible through a policy of equal opportunity. The very notion of a "gay version" here only tends to analogize gay experience to the structure of its own thereby all the more deeply denied oppression. And if the politics of this symmetrizing notion entail expunging all social precariousness from gay relations (along with every social reason for it), the aesthetics don't fail to register the same precariousness as so much formal impoverishment. Bound to be always invoking the presidence of heterosexual paradigms, but without benefit of the myth of life-process that makes the latter cohere in what Barthes calls "le naturel *social*," the gay version never ceases to convey its own factitiousness in the comparison, not unlike one of those wedding ceremonies where the couple writes their own service, as though to conceal from themselves the compulsory character of the ritual whose established phrasing—"man and wife!"—peals none the less through their clunking but forgettable modifications.

At its best, therefore, gay fabulation, even or especially before it became altogether visible as such, has been inseparable from a series of experiments needing to tamper with the most deeply imprinted aspects of traditional narrative form. If with his famously inconclusive conclusions, for instance, Gide may be thought to inaugurate the whole twentieth-century interrogation of narrative closure, he must also be seen as promoting that interrogation under the acknowledged pressure of a desire to whose call the endpoints of marriage and family-foundation, though remaining capable of keeping it on hold, fail in any less disspiriting way to respond. Or again, not the least marvellous effect of the myth of *le temps retrouvé* in Proust lies in its democratizing ability to extend the distribution of the traditional novel's most potent nutriment—I mean, that sense of life's richness whose usual allocation only goes to show that the rich get richer—to subjectivities estranged from the generation of marriage plots and to sexualities exceeding or falling short of the organization of the couple. And among the most important latter-day deviations from what can well appear the *nature* of narrative, there is every reason, including the profusion of his intertextual relations with Proust and Gide alike, to number Barthes's own narratology, as not just promoting an experimental narrative practice but constituting one as well.

In the days when the structural analysis of narrative obsessed criticism, Barthes produced the only narratology to transcend its overall grim technicity, the only one with a discernible animus. Even at its most laden with formal apparatus (which it yet carried so lightly, almost swishily), this narratology never rested content with assembling a catalogue raisonné of narrative units, functions, and modes, like its now unreadable rivals; or rather, in doing so, it took malicious aim at the whole ethos of the Novel established on the presumed naturalness of its narrative notations and stabilized by their presumed coherence. Hence, the twin tasks undertaken in *S/Z*: on the one hand, by evincing the artifice of signifying procedures at work throughout the classic realist text, to render what one may have been used to considering their natural operation as fully weird as anything that one may have been prepared to call *un*natural; and on the other, in calling attention to the abundant mere opinionativeness that stands behind the verisimilitude of such procedures, to reveal the source of the text's solidarity (with itself, with "life") in the self-contradicting consensus of *idées reçues*. Both tasks are meant to be advanced by the various discursive pulverizations (lexias, codes, charts, digressions) that not only break up Balzac's text, the better to dispel the illusion of a nature where "everything holds together," but also fragment Barthes's own analysis, so as to prevent the reconstitution of this illusion in the very demonstration of it.

Eventually in Barthes's career, however, this rigorous dilapidation of classic narrative, inevitably holding the critic to a libidinal dependency on what he loves-to-hate, evolves into a far less merely reactive cultivation of the resulting detritus—into a (reading or writing) practice of the Novel that chooses to be indifferent to overall architectonics and instead pursues effects whose smallness, flatness even, makes precisely for their value: an incident dislodged from the teleology of plot; a gesture excised from the consistency of character; a turn of phrase set to drift far beyond the practical exigencies of information or function. Of the many names Barthes uses to invoke this practice (the incident, the haiku, the biographeme), one is perhaps entitled to prefer *the novelesque without the novel* as best suggesting how intimately the still-resounding narrative accomplishment of *A Lover's Discourse*, *Roland Barthes*, *Camera Lucida*, or almost any of the late texts is conditional on the recognition and embrace of a certain privation. If in the very course of publishing toothsome excerpts from his journal, Barthes confirms the impossibility of his ever keeping a journal "with a view to publication," or if with no less theatricality he announces his preparations for writing a novel that he must have needed considerable discipline never actually to begin, it is that only by flirting—by *only* flirting—with the great narrative genres (of which the very greatest here—the Gidean Journal, the Proustian Novel—remain too gross) may the novelesque emerge in its radical askesis. For to so distinctively spare a practice as the novelesque, the least accommodating host accords perforce the friendliest abode. Congenial narrative forms inevitably risk reabsorbing the novelesque into the same large structural units (plot, character, theme) from whose immediate cultural stereotyping it proposes a provisional withdrawal, and so killing it with kindness; only a form that, by a sort of generic intolerance, admits narrative in the most parsimonious and finely milled doses is suited to resist (if only by retarding) the automatic accumulation of narrative in already read paradigms. Hence what is arguably the most interesting modern experiment in narrative minimalism finds its laboratory in, of all places, the *critical essay*, which Barthes urges to avow itself "almost a novel."

Why has this injunction been hardly heeded and Barthes's example seldom followed? The present critical terrain reveals two obvious lines of resistance, the one drawn around the discursive object, so that it may appear to exist in complete independence from whatever phantasmatics are in fact contributing to its elaboration; and the other cordoning off the discoursing subject, lest his presumed or desired autonomy be lost upon his becoming, as Barthes says of himself in his autobiography, "a character in a novel." If the academy sustains the first defense by the old stipulation of impersonality, it entrusts the second to the lately emergent counterpractice—having only had to forfeit some urgency to become as much at home in the conventional mainstream as on the contestatory margins—known as the personal. In contrast to the radical porousness of the novelesque subject, who as a character is always—indeed is only—open to being read through another's interpretative desire, the personal subject, divesting himself of all acknowledged fictiveness, communicates with us under the imperturbable assumption that he is who he thinks (refusal of the unconscious) and means as he chooses (refusal of the social and of language). That we seldom fail to receive with reverence, or at least in a respect-signifying hush, what manner and matter both let us call his *confidence* indicates the irresistible tendency of so protected, so untouchable, a subject to acquire sacred status—which is also to say, as every churchgoer might know, to inspire tedium, terror, and the iconoclasm of precisely such practices as the novelesque. Even in the openly autobiographical mode of *Roland Barthes*, the novelesque offers the spectacle of its willingness to trade the self-appointed securities of the personal for the disorienting effects—of intermittence, plurality, violation, exhaustion—produced on the subject by the principle of aberration that Barthes terms the Text (a designation that, though otherwise and elsewhere abstracting, might here enjoy the pertinence of reminding us how better borne the personal is in hearing than in reading). And yet, if the novelesque is postmodern enough to embrace the project of "decentering the subject," postmodern enough to be embraced by the critique of this project as itself thoughtlessly glamourizing the social-economic organization that lubricates our blithe mobility among contradictions—in short, if the theory of the novelesque enjoys such fashionable currency, then the question remains: Why is the novelesque still so comparatively rare a practice? The personal has been rightly claimed as a politics, well aimed at an impersonality that by occluding its own specificities of sex, race, class, gender, raises them into seeming universality; but the development of whatever political case might be argued for the self-chastisement and self-explosiveness performed in the name of the novelesque would have to start from the fact that to its few open practitioners the novelesque has value mainly as an erotics. Albeit much notice has been taken of the extreme pathos in late Barthes, sometimes to deplore his breach of old-fashioned decorum, more often to distinguish him for newer-fashioned bravery, none of it has succeeded in getting beyond its disgust or its sentimentality to recognize what kind of erotics this is. Barthes's own nonrecognition: "F. W. announces that one of these days I'll have to explain myself about the rejected aspects of my sexuality (in this case, sadomasochism), about which I never speak; I feel a certain irritation at this; to begin with, in strict logic, how could I explain myself about what does not exist?" (At which I find myself protesting, *but don't take it personally*.)

Broken Heart

To notice that on the sleeve of his writing hand the author of *A Lover's Discourse* wears a broken heart is also to acknowledge how well it suits him, quickening his perceptions of the world to the point of brilliance and almost directly mandating the urbanity, as dry as eyes having wept or clothes after wringing, of his prose: too well for its intimated suffering to be understood at face value. By the time of "Soirées de Paris" (to take of the elegiac note accompanying all Barthes's late writing the last and most confessional performance), his broken heart's redemption by worldly competencies has acquired the clarity of a schema. Let a hustler's rejection of the Pierrot-like diarist be a case in point: "I gave him some money, he promised to be at the rendezvous an hour later, and of course never showed." Barthes's rendering of—unlike the hustler's behavior in— the pathetic episode doesn't miss a trick, including the one that consists in *trying not to mind* the pain of which he thus makes us painfully mindful: "I asked myself if I was really so mistaken (the received wisdom about giving money to a hustler *in advance!*), and concluded that since I really didn't want him all that much (nor even to make love), the result was the same: sex or no sex, at eight o'clock I would find myself back at the same point in my life." Yet all such pathos is attended by a sophistication that (having absorbed just enough affective texture not to seem "brittle") manages, mitigates, and makes up for it, as almost immediately as the naïveté of paying a hustler "*in advance!*" becomes the knowing certainty that "of course" he wouldn't show. For the point at which, sex or no sex, Barthes again finds himself—fully at home, one might add—proves to be the worldly theatre par excellence, the Café de Flore, "where later in the evening, not far from our table, another hustler . . ."

No sorry adventure of Barthes's Parisisan nights seems complete without his repairing to the celebrated terrace that is part society meeting place, part gay cruising ground, and part intellectual sanctum for reflecting on Pascal or reading a newspaper with no news; in which combination, the Flore not only sends Barthes forth to the hustlers across the boulevard, or refreshes him on his return from particular hotels and saunas further afield, but also presents a thought-coaxing annex to his workspace, whose eventual products will be negotiated, celebrated, discussed here as well. Much as in the late-seventies disco, lovesick lyrics would provoke dancing that was anything but crestfallen, so at this site Barthes's contemporary sorrows manifest their destiny in recalling him to the world and recathecting him to the worldly virtues of irony and savoir faire, whose written practice will always have meant more to him than the simple sexual act that, though manqué, is scarcely missed. Who then cannot feel what Barthes only pretends to ignore: the euphoria that gladdens his most morose mood as soon as he sets foot on the Flore's sidewalk? (Not I, who forget to pity Barthes his troubles so much do I envy him their scene—now changed, with the hustlers gone, the Dragon closed, and so forth, but oh, even last year, what thrill of passion, of knowledge, when I rose from my table at the Flore, crossed the boulevard, and—finally making proper use of the Drugstore—bought Steve a toothbrush!)

Yet it is no less true that Barthes's very efforts to induce his unhappiness—evenhandedly ranging from the hustler he pays beforehand to the *bécébégé* boyfriend he sends away at the end, saying he has work to do—can only compromise the worldly ethos that is supposed to absorb them but whose perfection can never admit of being thus worked at. It begins to appear as though the entire redemptive protocol possessed only the hopeful reality of a fantasy scenario, as studiously repeated as a sex act in pornography and for the same reason: to demonstrate against abiding doubt that it can actually occur. What finally governs the writing of "Soirées" is less a complacent relation to the broken heart (whose motto might be Barthes's telling remark on finding the Keller bar: "relieved, we gave up") than a fear lest, like an engine in the cold, the broken heart should refuse to *turn over* and suffer fracture of a different order: fracture that would not be the result of any given loss, but of the drastic inhibition of whatever psychic energies might register or respond to that loss. Death is doubled when, after the decease of someone I love, I suddenly comprehend that the person to whom in my grief I have thought of turning (he will know how to console me, remember with me) is the very person who has just died. It is the universalization of this predicament that impends over the author of "Soirées," whose mother's death, spreading spillwise over the whole state of his affairs, continually threatens to become the death of "the" mother and so to achieve the absoluteness of a loss that would include any capacity to recover from it. The journal-writing thus anticipates—impossible to decide whether to confirm or contest—the prospect of losing "even" a broken heart to a deadened affect that would make life-giving dramatizations of loss no longer possible.

The ritual charge levelled against ACT UP!—that its militants are too chic, its meetings too cruisy, and manifestations too theatrical—could thus instead be seen to point to an achievement whose precise measure of difficulty the impasse reached by Barthes's broken heart allows us to take. For even as, relative to the catastrophe enveloping it, the broken heart comes to see the falseness of its petty-little-problems, it also understands, relative to the same catastrophe, that it must be further than ever from any wish to give up their sustenance. Torn by contempt for what it will not do without, it only settles matters through a self-trivialization that preserves it at the price of preventing it from taking its pleasures seriously, or feeling its unpleasures strongly. Barthes's self-portrait in "Soirées" oscillates accordingly between two modes of diminution: cliché and crankiness; if the former internalizes the absoluteness of death in the stereotype (the Sad Old Queen), the latter protests this reduction with nothing better than the mere prickliness of individuality ("why should you think I like your music, would go out of my way to see your movie?"). And in this state of self-doubt, where it no longer pays to have, say, the mortification of having to pay, the broken heart ceases to provide the spring and support for the transfigurations of *style*, and its only sufficiently inadequate correlative becomes the "immediate" writing of the intimate journal. (Like a body that necessity has compelled to abandon the gym, Barthes's last writing is by turns shamefaced, defiant, or uncaring on the question of how it looks. Like that body, it may provoke pitiful, reproachful, "turned off" responses—from all perhaps except those who have most fully embraced it as body: they are its lovers.) Under such and so much pressure, the broken heart veers toward the breakdown adumbrated, though never accomplished, at the end of "Soirées": toward the question that Barthes knows must be answered, but can do no more than simply pose: "Quel sera pour moi le spectacle du monde?" What will the world's spectacle come to be for me?

Alone and a little lonely in a new town, I met a man who, with the kindness of strangers, proposed a Sunday drive; en route, whether just to make conversation, or perhaps with the design of establishing the degrees and kinds of his availability, he began recounting an episode of long and ungrateful obsession with a man who had once rejected him. Ready enough for sociability, I met his story with a similar one of my own, details of which I would interject into the course of his, in what mutually stimulating disclosure soon made a sort of potlatch, producing greater hilarity as deeper humiliations were sacrificed to our developing bond—but eventually reaching this frigorific climax when I happened to mention my beloved by name: "But *I* knew Ralph. He's dead."

To an announcement that still leaves me nothing to say or feel—nothing, I mean, respecting epidemic proportion—the last text of Roland Barthes affords a precious little reverberation. For that reason too, I dream of bringing him back.

Designer:	Sandy Drooker
Compositor:	Wilsted & Taylor
Text:	11/13.5 Fournier
Display:	Fournier
Printer:	Malloy Lithographing
Binder:	Malloy Lithographing

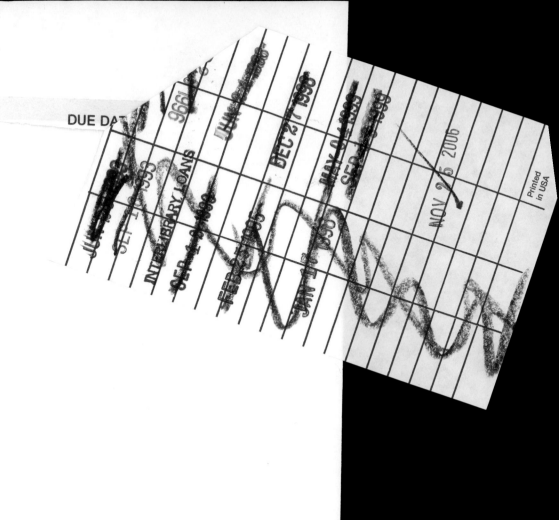

DUE DATE